POWER

BOLAND

POWER & AUTHORITY MATTER TO GOD

POWER & AUTHORITY MATTER TO GOD, by John W. Boland. All rights reserved. (2022)

Published in the United states of America
ISBN: 9798839006461
Imprint: Independently published

1. Nonfiction > Religion > Christianity > General
2. Nonfiction > Religion > Religion, Politics & State

TABLE OF CONTENTS

BOLAND

INTRODUCTION

*The very arrogance of the Pharisees
to ask Jesus...by what authority do you do
these things? Who gave you this authority?*
Matthew 21:23b

Does power and authority really matter to God? The answer is yes! It matters because it belongs to Him and no one else. The Bible makes something perfectly clear at the start...all power and authority belong to God. There is no question about that.[i]

- God created the heavens and the earth.[ii]
- God created light.[iii]
- God created day and night.[iv]
- God created the land and the water.[v]
- God created vegetation, plants, and trees.[vi]
- God created all living creatures.[vii]
- God created man.
  - The original Hebrew word for 'man' is 'Adam' {אדם} and the word for 'ground' is 'Adamah' {אדמה}, because "the LORD God formed the man of dust from the ground and breathed into his nostrils the breath of life, and the man became a living creature."[viii]
- God created woman
  - The English word Eve became her name when mispronounced from a Vulgate bible translation. Her name was originally הַוָּה (*chava*) in Hebrew, which has a root connection with a verb לִחְיוֹת (*lichyot*) "to live", and words such as חַי (chai) and חַיִּים (*chayim*) communicating the idea of "life."[ix]

The term "human beings" comes from the Hebrew *'Benei Adam'* {בני אדם} which literally means 'the children of Adam' because of the strong biblical foundation of the Hebrew culture believing that all the people in the world are direct descendants of Adam and Eve.

Job tells us that God's power caused the earth to hang on nothing in the void of space. Even though Job did not know what he was talking about.[x] Isaiah saw the same thing. He saw God's power sitting high above the earth making all humanity appear to be a speck in the vastness of creation.[xi] God even posed the questions for us through His servant Isaiah:

- Who created the heavens?   God!
- Who formed the earth and made it? God!
- Who created it to be inhabited?   God!

The disciple John puts an exclamation point on the idea of God's power and authority by stating that,

> *"All things were made through Him,*
> *and without Him was not anything made*
> *that was made."*[xii]

God said very clearly,

> *"I AM the Lord, and there is no other!*[xiii]

So, how does God's power and authority relate to us? How does it affect us? Since God created man in His image has some of that power and authority rubbed off? What about man's use and misuse of power and authority over the course of history? How does all that play into God's ultimate power and authority?

POWER &
AUTHORITY
RECOGNIZED

*In the beginning God created
the heaven and the earth.*

Genesis 1:1

FACTS ACKNOWLEDGED

Scripture established that God is the only source of power and authority. He created the structure of everything from the family, the church, the workplace, and finally the rules of society. In the Old Testament, it wasn't until God spoke through Moses that He made it clear that He wanted a relationship with each and every one of us. He also wanted that relationship to be passed on throughout society by various personal interactions such as one to one conversations, family interactions, community involvement, and the workplace. He clearly established how we could ruin that relationship with Him and others. We now recognize these as the "Ten Commandments."[xiv]

The New Testament declares that we should pay attention to our relationships. These relationships include our spouse, parents, children, friends, enemies, neighbors strangers, orphans, widows, and with the governing authorities of the day.[xv] This last one is because all their power and authority is

God ordained, the good, the bad, and even the ugly. It is in these organizations that we see God's orderliness, or man's lack thereof, the difference is easy to observe. In Jesus' life, He set the example for us to follow by regularly deferring and yielding to the will, the power, and authority of God rather than pursuing a personal agenda.[xvi] Jesus was obedient to death!

God's design for mankind was not that of political power, ideological divisions, racism, or partisanship. God's design for mankind is for an eternal Spiritual relationship with Him through Jesus Christ which is outwardly expressed in those relationships we have with others.[xvii] As the Triune God (Father, Son, and Holy Spirit) works within their power and authority structure, they affect human governmental authorities to fulfill their specific role. The Triune God perfectly completes and reveals the glory of God. Therefore, if we fit into the plans of God, we are not free of each other. In other words, as members of a family, church, or society, we are not independent of one another. We are dependent on each other and the authority of God. It is He Who directs and empowers the Son and Holy Spirit to carry out His Will. It is He who establishes order in society. It is He who keeps the world from falling into chaos! God has established human authority in the following four areas:

1. The Family[xviii],
2. The Community[xix],
3. The Religious[xx],
4. The Economy[xxi].

Scripture establishes a specific order in each of those areas. These structures do not establish any one person or group as dominant over others. Each organization is fulfilled through the servanthood of individuals within each grouping.[xxii] Just as the Triune God is diverse and complete so too are the social structures and chains of command within these areas. These different components are essential for the success of the relationships within them[xxiii]. As we shall see later.

What we must understand is that everyone of us is accountable for our own actions. We are accountable to each other for the overall success! No matter if we are in authority or not. God cares less what culture you have, what education level you attained, what position you hold, or how wealthy you are. God judges each person according to "His righteous standards" not yours or mine.[xxiv]

Accountability is the basis on which all relationships depend. As believers,

- Parents are accountable to God and society for their children,
- Children are accountable to God and their parents for their conduct,
- Employees are accountable to their employers for their work ethos,
- Employers are accountable to owners, corporations, and/or the law for ethics,
- Citizens are accountable to the communities for orderliness and lawfulness.

Each of us must carry out our individual responsibilities. As we do this our relationship with God, or lack thereof, can be seen in how we relate to others.[xxv] Human authorities are accountable to God and each of us. They are accountable for how they exercise their time in power.[xxvi] They are responsible to provide protection, direction, safety, and care. They are to punish those who do wrong, and to praise those who do well.[xxvii] We are all accountable to God for how we respond to those under our authority and above us on the authority food chain. We are therefore to submit to God's design and His authority in our lives.[xxviii]

When a society, culture, or nation experiences periods of chaos, confusion, division, distress, or civil strife the problem is simple. The majority have walked away from their relationship with God almighty and decided to live on their own without Him. Those in power and authority have decided to create laws that are not in line with God's standards. It is those decisions that have brought on the conflict, division and strife that they experience. Remember "decisions have consequences."[xxix]

BIBLE STUDY

Deuteronomy 27:26
> Cursed be he that confirmeth not all the words of this law to do them. And all the people shall say, Amen.

Deuteronomy 28:1-2
> It shall come to pass, if thou shalt hearken diligently unto the voice of the Lord thy God, to observe and to do all his commandments which I command thee this day, that the Lord thy God will set thee on high above all nations of the earth: And all these blessings shall come on thee, and overtake thee, if thou shalt hearken unto the voice of the Lord thy God.

Romans 13:1
> Let every soul be subject unto the higher powers. For there is no power but of God: the powers that be are ordained of God.

Matthew 28:18
> Jesus came and spoke unto them, saying, All power is given unto me in heaven and in earth.

Matthew 20:25-28

> Jesus called them unto him, and said, You know that the princes of the Gentiles exercise dominion over them, and they that are great exercise authority upon them. But it shall not be so among you but whosoever will be great among you, let him be your minister and whosoever will be chief among you, let him be your servant. Even as the Son of man came not to be ministered unto, but to minister, and to give his life a ransom for many.

Daniel 4:17

> This matter is by the decree of the watchers, and the demand by the word of the holy ones: to the intent that the living may know that the most High rules in the kingdom of men, and giveth it to whomsoever He will, and sets up over it the basest of men.

Please answer the following questions:
- Who established power and authority over man?
- How can we be "subject" to those in power and authority
- What is the consequences of not being in line with God's power and authority?

POWER

FACTS CONFIRMED

The Family

Whether we want to admit it or not, God entrusted leadership of the family unit to the male (husband). He is assigned to love his female (wife) as himself! That unfortunately is a tall order in this day and age, especially when Satanical forces have introduced such things as "gay marriage", and "gender confusion". A wife is to submit (defer) to the leadership of her husband. This means to come alongside as a "helpmate."[xxx] It does not mean be under or behind. When the children come along, they (both), as parents, are responsible to train up their children according to God's order (not an individual's order or a group's order). The children are to honor and obey their parents.[xxxi]

Whether we want to admit or not we are seeing the breakdown of the family which is leading to the breakdown of society. One area is in the male's failure to take responsibility for the family. Whether the relationship is legal or not. I am not talking about a sexual encounter with a prostitute, but the ever more common young person who allows their hormones to overrule their brains and have premarital sex.[xxxii] God's plan for human reproduction is for the male and female to be legally married in His eyes. However, in our age of premarital encounters if a child is created, abortion should not be an option. The male has a responsibility for the upbringing of the child along with the female.[xxxiii]

Government has illegitimately undermined family values with such programs as child support, welfare, food stamps etc. Governments have encouraged and brought about the breakdown of the core family. These well-meaning but evil programs have taken away the dependence of the family on the father figure. These government programs stripped the church from giving a hand up and helping in Jesus name in lieu of a dependence on a regular government handout. Dependence on government has given rise to atheism, political extremism, agnosticism, satanism, LGTBQ, self-mutilation in the name of freedom, and the murdering of the unborn on demand. All of which the church has failed to combat effectively.

- God's people, through their leadership, have yielded biblical power and authority to illegitimate government programs which are not based on scripture.

- God's people lost the battle for family values and stability due to soft preaching and the inability to understand scripture.

- God's people gave up helping the truly needy and assisting true widows to a godless government because they do not know scripture.

- God's people have turned over the church liturgy to the liberal culture because they do not know scripture.

- God's people have accepted the promotion of the unrepentant to leadership positions within the church body because they do not know scripture.

- God's people have no place in praying for the clinics or those who perform abortions.

- God's people who see nothing wrong with doing any of this are not true believers and do not know scripture..[xxxiv]

The Community

God's original intent was that human's follow God, God's order, and God's prophets. Scripture instructs us to respect and obey such authority and ordinances. It goes on to instruct us to live honorably within our communities. Leaders and local officials are to punish those who do wrong and honor those who do well.[xxxv] It is not God's intention that officials "play favorites."[xxxvi] It is not God's intention that officials rule forever.[xxxvii] God knew humans were prone to violence, corruption, and evil.[xxxviii] Therefore, humans need order, structure, and direction.

In the Old Testament we see that the ultimate structural view of humankind is found in the prophetic utterances of the person of the Messiah.[xxxix] That is why the Old Testament texts concerning creation are fully implemented in the mystery of restoration of life and salvation. The Biblical texts go on to say that we are all aware of our internal dependence on God. However, it further shows our desire toward self-determination, and selfishness which naturally pushes us away from that dependence on God. This love–hate relationship with God has its source in something internal dating back to Adam's experience in the garden. At that moment Adam knew his situation, he knew his condition, he knew his position, he knew his need, yet he denied the truth after acquiring the knowledge.[xl]

Psychology professor Abraham H. Maslow put a name to this. He called it the *"hierarchy of needs."* This theory states that humans have five-tier levels of basic requirements for life. He created a hierarchical pyramid to illustrate this theory. From the bottom of the hierarchy upwards, the needs are:

- Physiological (Food And Clothing),
- Safety (Job Security),
- Love And Belonging (Friendship),
- Self-Esteem (Confidence),
- Self-Actualization (Potential).[xli]

The Religious

God created us for a one-to-one individual personal relationship not for corporate worship. Jesus railed against the hypocrisy of Jewish leaders who misled the people by restricting the people's access to God, and misinterpreting God's Word. Jesus came alongside each person and established a church that was supposed to be run by a host of individuals based on their Spiritual Gifts (i.e.: the Body of Christ) not a corporate religious hierarchy. The church is dependent upon Spiritually Gifted leadership of administrators, elders, and teachers. These individuals are essential for the health of the body. However, all the Spiritual Gifts must be exercised equally in order for the world to see God glorified and honored in an appropriate way. Believers are to honor and respect leaders, submit one to another, and walk in humility.[xlii]

The Economy

In the area of business, employers are called upon to act with impartiality and watchfulness as they oversee those they employ.[xliii] They should establish their behavior patterns based on the Scriptures.[xliv] We must all remember that God is their authority.[xlv] Those employed should serve well, also do their best work, and give wholeheartedly as unto the Lord.[xlvi] Let's look at the facts:

- God placed man on earth for work.[xlvii]
- God blessed each of us with skills to do every sort of work from the mundane to the exceptional.[xlviii]
- God wants His people to be engaged in their economy.[xlix]
- God wants His people to be honest in their business dealings all the time.[l]
- God wants His people to treat others fairly and justly.[li]

BIBLE STUDY

Romans 13:1 ESV
>   Let every soul be subject unto the higher powers. For there is no power but of God: the powers that be are ordained of God.

Ephesians 5:23
>   For the husband is the head of the wife, as Christ is the head of the church and He is the savior of the body.

Daniel 2:38
>   Wheresoever the children of men dwell, the beasts of the field and the fowls of the heaven hath He given into thine hand, and hath made thee ruler over them all...

James 1:27
>   Pure religion and undefiled before God and the Father is this, to visit the fatherless and widows in their affliction, and to keep oneself unspotted from the world.

Ecclesiastes 5:10 ESV
>   He who loves money will not be satisfied...nor he who loves wealth with his income...

Please answer the following questions:
- What do these verses say about the power and authority God turned over to humans?
- What limitations do you see?

POWER

BOLAND

POWER &
AUTHORITY
CHALLENGED

God said, "Hear my words:
If there is a prophet among you,
I the Lord make myself known to him
in a vision; I speak with him in a dream.

Numbers 12:6

PARADISE LOST

Originally, God set up human beings to rule over the earth under His power and authority. We were to live in paradise forever. From the very moment humans were created, we became stewards, not owners of the environment. We became responsible for how things turn out, yet we are not to worship this moving mass as a goddess or deity. We are to take care of it.

Adam and Eve thought they were more than caretakers and did not listen to the instructions of God and lost paradise. Just as Adam and Eve listened to the lies around them, people today are being fooled by listening to the same old lies and losing their joy.[lii] Adam and Eve's son Cain thought it was beneath him to worship God appropriately. Cain, in a fit of jealousy, because his brothers gift was more acceptable, lashed out and killed him. Just as Cain had contempt for God, people today both in and out of the church are conducting themselves contemptibly toward things of God. Just as Cain mistrusted God's purpose and meaning, today's culture thinks it beneath them to understand God's ways. The current culture has the same attitude as Cain, one of jealousy toward the relationship that believers have with God and will lash out, ridicule, and attempt to humiliate God's people every chance they get. The current culture think that they are:

- Sophisticated,
  - o It is beneath them to worship a creator God.
- Advanced,
  - o in the age of technology, reading "that book" is not worth their time.
- Intellectual,
  - o They will not be controlled by myths and an unseen deity.
- Mature,
  - o Those respected by society do not consider outdated standards.
- Educated,
  - o An academic does not believe in such pointless words.

The current culture says that God's Words are exclusive, bigoted, and homophobic.

BOLAND

BIBLE STUDY

Genesis 2:16-17, 3:6, 23-24

The Lord God commanded the man, saying, Of every tree of the garden thou mayest freely eat but of the tree of the knowledge of good and evil, thou shalt not eat of it: for in the day that thou eat thereof thou shalt surely die... So, when the woman saw that the tree was good for food, and that it was pleasant to the eyes, and a tree to be desired to make one wise, she took of the fruit thereof, and did eat, and gave also unto her husband with her; and he did eat. Therefore the Lord God sent him forth from the garden of Eden, to till the ground from whence he was taken. So he drove out the man; and he placed at the east of the garden of Eden Cherubim, and a flaming sword which turned every way, to keep the way of the tree of life.

Genesis 4:4-5, 8

Abel, he also brought of the firstlings of his flock and of the fat thereof. And the Lord had respect unto Abel and to his offering. But unto Cain and to his offering he had not respect. And Cain was very wroth, and his countenance fell.

Cain talked with Abel his brother: and it came to pass, when they were in the field, that Cain rose up against Abel his brother, and slew him.

Please answer the following questions:
- What lost paradise for Adam and Eve?
  - Was it Attitude? Conduct? Action?
- Why did Cain take the action he did?
  - Was it Attitude? Conduct? Jealousy?

POWER

AUTHORITY CHALLENGED

Just because the building where you meet on Sunday has a religious or biblical name does not give it authority to speak for God. Just because you have a cross in the building, religious pictures on the wall, or windows, does not mean anyone in that place is authorized to speak in Jesus name. Just because someone wears religious jewelry does not mean Jesus is Lord of their life.[liii] Nor does . it mean that Jesus is Lord of the life of someone who has a degree from a seminary either!

In Jesus day there were leaders who could only read scripture, and then there were those who were authorized to preach. The synagogue at Capernaum where Jesus went and taught was led by scribes. These individuals could only read the Word of God in the synagogue gatherings so the people were exposed to the truth of God. These same scribes did not have the power or authority to interpret the Word of God. Only a true rabbi had authority to interpret the Word. So, it was obvious that "church leaders" would challenge Jesus authority to preach, heal, and do miracles in "God's name".[liv]

Humanity, from the very beginning of time have taken "God's Word" out of context, even those authorized to interpret it! Individuals, groups, even organizations have misinterpreted the very meaning of God's Word. They attempt to put Him in a nice, neat package with a bow on it in order to suit their agenda.

From almost the very beginning of the writing down of the scriptures, humanity has challenged God's authority, law, and declarations.

1. Satan challenged God in the garden of Eden.

2. The people of Babylon thought they could build a tower reaching into the heavens. They tried to show God who they were.[lv]

3. In Genesis 18 Abraham challenged God's declaration to destroy Sodom and Gomorrah.[lvi]

4. In Exodus 32 Moses challenged God's decision to deal with the people when they built the calf after 40 days with Moses being absent.

5. In the book of Amos, twice, Amos pleads with God, and twice God relents after God announces judgement on Israel in two visions.[lvii]

6. There are other examples of men challenging God throughout scripture.[lviii]

Individual's throughout history believed they have received a word from God which clearly contradicts the true Word of God. Unfortunately, many have the charisma, necessary resources, and communicative skills to make themselves believable. At some point, they may feel they have been ignored and break away. They will take steps to challenge the status quo to a disastrous end. Modern examples are:

- The Peoples Temple (1955-1978),
- The Branch Davidians (1955-1993),
- Sullivanians (1957-1991),
- Children of God – Family International (1968-Present),
- Heaven's Gate (1972-1997)

BIBLE STUDY

Genesis 11:1-4, 8
> The whole earth was of one language, and of one speech...they said, Go to, let us build us a city and a tower, whose top may reach unto heaven; and let us make us a name, lest we be scattered abroad upon the face of the whole earth... So the Lord scattered them abroad from thence upon the face of all the earth: and they left off to build the city.

Genesis 18:20-26
> The Lord said, because the cry of Sodom and Gomorrah is great, and because their sin is very grievous... Abraham drew near, and said, Wilt thou also destroy the righteous with the wicked?

Exodus 32:9-11
> The Lord said unto Moses, I have seen this people, and behold, it is a stiff-necked people. Now therefore let me alone, that my wrath may wax hot against them, and that I may consume them: and I will make of thee a great nation... Moses besought the Lord his God, and said, Lord, why doth thy wrath wax hot against thy people, which thou hast brought forth out of the land of Egypt with great power, and with a mighty hand?

Please answer the following questions:
- Is it ever appropriate to question God's power and authority?
- If there an appropriate time to question God?
  - If so, when is it?

POWER

POWER CHALLENGED

"Jealousy" is thinking, you want what others have. This sickness seems to drive human beings into making irrational decisions which increase with what we call the crowd mentality. What seems to be left out of their reasoning is that decisions (no matter good or bad) have consequences. What probably started within a conversation between two people, increased among one tribe of Israelites and was catapulted into a shouting match of

"we want to be just like other people,
therefore, give us a king!"

God, through Moses, had led these people from slavery to national identity. He led them out of repression to revival. He took them from labor to life. Yet, they were not content with the organizational structure established by God. These people didn't want God's chosen prophet. They wanted to be led by royalty rather than a deity. They wanted to feel just like everyone else not a separate and distinct people with a mission purpose. They wanted to be just like everyone else![lix]

God separated out the descendants of Abraham, Isaac, and Jacob for a particular function of serving Him and being His witnesses before the world.[lx] God wanted them to become a model nation before a corrupt world.[lxi] God wanted them to show the rest of the world His way of life. God wanted them to share His blessings with others who would turn to Him too. God would bring forth the Messiah from this group of people.[lxii] God made it clear to the people of Israel that it wasn't because "they" were anything special but it was their connection to Abraham.[lxiii] Yet, as privileged as they were, they fought their future, they denounced their blessing, time and again.

Ever since that change from prophet to politics, the religious and political leaders have not demonstrated a relationship with God as Moses did.[lxiv] Yet, God commands us to respect the authority of all leaders,

"for there is no authority except from God."[lxv]

This does not mean we should never question them. This does not mean we should not hold them accountable, or even replace them. It does mean that whenever we have a grievance against those in legitimate authority our duty is to discern their ways, their conduct, and their decisions as it relates to God's power and authority. We are to respect the position.[lxvi]

In scripture Jesus power and authority was questioned by those jealous of Him. They were not seeking to justify that power and authority but were hoping to trap Him. They were looking for blasphemy, if He claimed that his authority came directly from God. They were looking for hypocrisy, if He claimed that the authority came from himself. Regardless of His defense, they merely want to humiliate, ridicule, and make Him appear foolish.[lxvii] That is what politicians do. They don't seek the real truth they seek to humiliate those they oppose and discredit them. Jesus was God's Son, and Samuel was God's representative both told the people God's truth. Those in politics do not want to hear that truth. They want to hear their version of the truth. God warned the people what would happen.[lxviii]

POWER

BIBLE STUDY

Exodus 19:3-5

Moses went up unto God, and the Lord called unto him out of the mountain, saying, Thus shalt thou say to the house of Jacob, and tell the children of Israel. You have seen what I did unto the Egyptians, and how I bare you on eagles' wings, and brought you unto myself. Now therefore, if you will obey my voice indeed, and keep my covenant, then you shall be a peculiar treasure unto me above all people: for all the earth is mine:

1 Samuel 8:4-5

Then all the elders of Israel gathered themselves together, and came to Samuel unto Ramah, and said unto him, Behold, thou art old, and thy sons walk not in thy ways: now make us a king to judge us like all the nations.

Please answer the following questions:
- Why is it so hard for humankind to follow God?
- Why is it that we would rather follow faulty fellow beings rather than a holy God?

POWER

GOD'S WARNING IGNORED

When the people cried out for a king, so that they would be like everyone else. God's Word came to Samuel. He then told them what the power and authority of a ruling class would look like: The ruling class would:

- Force Military Service on future generations.
- Force Labor on future generations for their Political Purposes.
- Create Unnecessary, Unwarranted, and Disproportionate Taxes on future generations.
- Take Private Property,
- Redistribute that Property among themselves and their friends.
- Create Unrestrained Political Power.[lxix]

God, through Samuel went on to say that when you have had enough of these leaders and you want relief from these ruling classes which "you wanted and cried out for," God the Lord will not hear your cries.[lxx]

So, what does all this mean? Consider the condition of history. The young lives sacrificed in the wars of the ruling classes throughout the old testament. The list of wars, rumors of wars, the lives wasted, and the time and lives spent defending arbitrary property lines called territories. These wars of "honor and alliances" of the ruling classes are what fills the pages of world history just as God warned through Samuel. If you just glance through history over time you can follow the multiple senseless wars and conquest by empires and empire want-to-bees. Wars of succession. Wars of rebellion and even peasant revolts. From 1096 through 1297 the Catholic church recruited and funded *The Crusades* for the return(?)/conquest of holy land from Muslim control (Jerusalem). Such conflicts could last from several days to many years (i.e.: 1337-1453 *The Hundred Years' War*).[lxxi]

However, in order to conduct these bloody conflicts the ruling class had to be able to raise and fund an army. That meant they had to force men into military service. This action is what we know as a draft. It is the process by which a government selects one or more individuals into compulsory service or forced enrollment into armed service. The first recorded conscription dated back to ancient Mesopotamia. In those days under the

Hammurabi Code[lxxii], Babylonian kingdoms employed a system of conscription called *ilkum,* in which laborers owed military service to royal officials for the right to own land. During the *Middle Ages* land peasants were often required to provide one man per family for military duty.

During the French Revolution (1790) the first modern draft occurred. The *Civil War* brought about the conscription process in United States which wasn't very well received to say the least.

Now no one can say that gathering men for service did not happen in the Old Testament. In the book of Numbers, God directed Moses and Aaron to take a census of all fighting age men twenty and older.[lxxiii]

BIBLE STUDY

1 Samuel 9-18

(God said) Now therefore hearken unto their voice: howbeit yet protest solemnly unto them and shew them the manner of the king that shall reign over them. Samuel told all the words of the Lord unto the people that asked of him a king. he said, This will be the manner of the king that shall reign over you:

- He will take your sons, and appoint them for himself, for his chariots, and to be his horsemen; and some shall run before his chariots.

- He will appoint him captains over thousands, and captains over fifties; and will set them to ear his ground, and to reap his harvest, and to make his instruments of war, and instruments of his chariots.

- He will take your daughters to be confectionaries, and to be cooks, and to be bakers.

- He will take your fields, and your vineyards, and your olive yards, even the best of them, and give them to his servants.

- He will take the tenth of your seed, and of your vineyards, and give to his officers, and to his servants.

- He will take your menservants, and your maidservants, and your

goodliest young men, and your asses, and put them to his work.
- He will take the tenth of your sheep: and you shall be his servants.

When you shall cry out in that day because of your king which you shall have chosen. The Lord will not hear you in that day.

Please answer the following questions:
- Why did the people not listen to God?
- Why do you think they insist on having a king?

POWER

RESULTS

God not only told us what power and authority in the hands of politicians would be like. He told us to respect those in charge who would do it to us! He said this because no one has been or will be in a position of authority, no one, without His full knowledge.[lxxiv] God has told us not to seek revenge on someone who has harmed us but let those in authority take care of the matter.[lxxv] God told us not to fear those in authority because they are there to punish those who break the law, not law-abiding citizens. Certainly, if this is not the case then they are of the devil not of God. However, in normal circumstances, if you're not breaking the law you have nothing to fear.[lxxvi] God told us to show ourselves to be respectful and honest before everyone.[lxxvii] Scriptures warned us that the art of living comes with trials, tribulation, pain, and problems with every new day.[lxxviii] Don't allow these things that befall us to overwhelm and beat you into the character of the godless secular world.[lxxix]

God said that those in authority should not lower themselves to using threats to get their way. They should not show partiality. They should not be prejudicial or biased in anyway but treat everyone fairly and just.[lxxx] Good, bad, or indifferent all persons of influence are put into their positions by God. Therefore, they are where they are for a time such as it is.[lxxxi] So when those in authority do not do things according to your standard, be patient with them. Do not use God as a crutch for your biases, attitude, or conduct.[lxxxii] By all means do not consider yourself the voice of the almighty.[lxxxiii] It was Jesus who declared that we should not put God to any test. Even if our cause is right in our eyes.[lxxxiv]

<u>Military Service:</u>

God predicted that those in power and authority would call the young people to military service. So, the development of what we now know as the selective service or draft is obviously nothing new.[lxxxv] Even God called men to fight for His purposes, His honor and His glory throughout scripture.[lxxxvi] In biblical times, all men aged twenty to 50 years old were able to go to war. They were required to defend the land and fight.[lxxxvii] Even King David blessed God for his ability to go to war.[lxxxviii] Consider just a few of the biblical wars:

- Conquest Wars (circa 1400-1550 B.C.)[lxxxix]
    - Battles of Jericho, Ai, Hazor & the Conquest of Canaan
- Battle of Gibeah (c. 1200-1000 b.c.)[xc]
- Gideon and the Midianites (c. 1184 b.c.)[xci]
- Wars of Saul (c. 1021-1100 b.c.)[xcii]

<u>Welfare</u>:

Throughout scripture God has direct "His people" to meet the needs of the fatherless, true widows, and strangers.[xciii] He has told us to be their encouragers, supporters, and promoters.[xciv] He even established the basic outline for what a true widow looks like:

- 70 years old (minimum)
- Wife of only one man,
- No family support available,
- No living children,
- Trusts God,
- Abandoned by family,
- Blameless in character.[xcv]

God's directive was designed to bring those in need into the fellowship of Godly believers. The help God designed was a temporary fix for a short-term situation, not a long-term dependency. Consider it a hand up not a handout. Consider then what those in modern power and authority have done to the fatherless, needy, unwed mothers, true widows, homeless and strangers. After the economic hard times of the 1930's more and more people moved to depend on government "welfare" (aid, assistance, or child support programs.). To many individuals, families and generations have become influenced by government money to exist, to have a living standard, and maintain their lifestyles. (homes, vehicles, phones, food, children, etc.) These people are more dependent on government money and political authorities than God ever intended.

BIBLE STUDY

Genesis 3:23

> The LORD God sent him (humans) forth from the garden of Eden, to till the ground from whence he was taken.

Genesis 11:4

> They (humans) said, let us build us a city and a tower, whose top may reach unto heaven and let us make us a name, lest we be scattered abroad upon the face of the whole earth.

1 Samuel 8:4-6

> All the elders of Israel gathered themselves and came to Samuel and said unto him, behold, thou art old, and thy sons walk not in thy ways. Now make us a king to judge just like all the nations.

1 Samuel 8:10, 11a, 18, 19

> Samuel told all the words of the Lord unto the people that asked of him a king. This will be the manner of the king that shall reign over you...
> Nevertheless the people refused to obey...
> So, when you cry out because of the king which you chose, the Lord will not hear you.

Matthew 22:21 ESV
> He (Jesus) said to them, "Therefore render to Caesar the things that are Caesar's, and to God the things that are God's."

Please answer the following questions;
- Based on these verses, what do you think about human tendencies toward power and authority?
- Can humankind ever just understand biblical truth and take God at His Word?
  - Why or why not?

POWER

BOLAND

POWER &
AUTHORITY
EXPOSED

He (Jesus) said to them,
The kings of the Gentiles
exercise lordship over them, and
those in authority over them are called
benefactors.

Luke 22:25 ESV

- God created His people with the power and authority to be His witness among the nations.[xcvi]
  - Although too many people fail to step out and attest to the influence of the Lord in their life.

- God created His people with the power and authority to overcome hate with love for Him and each other.[xcvii]
  - Although too many people fail to show how love overcomes hate in their daily lives.

- God created His people with the power and authority to overcome their enemies.[xcviii]
  - Although too many people fail to believe God and simply accept defeat in the face of victory.

- God created His people with the power and authority to overcome their weakest moments.[xcix]
  - Although too many people allow their weakness to overcome their God given power and authority.

- God created His people with the power and authority to overcome anything man-made by His Word.[c]
  - Although too many people fail to read, study, memorize, meditate, or consider His Word.

- God created His people with the power and authority to overcome the folly of the secular lies with biblical truth.[ci]
  - Although too many people fail to consider biblical truth when confronted by secular lies.

- God created His people with the power and authority to communicate with Him in order to bring honor and glory to His name.[cii]
  - Although too many people fail to understand the effectiveness, appropriateness, and proper approach to prayer.

- God created His people with the power and authority to achieve great things for His honor and glory.[ciii]
  - Although too many people fail to achieve anything because they pursue self-interests over God's Will.[civ]

- God created His people with the power and authority to establish an example of self-control before the secular world.[cv]
  - Although too many people fail to believe in the name of Jesus Christ because they believe the secular lies and have not fully read the scriptural accounts of success.[cvi]

SELF-GOVERNING

Self-Control

God created His people with the power and authority to overcome selfishness through self-control. A person who lacks self-control is like a defenseless city.[cvii] God has always directed us to have a strong will power. We are to be quick to hear, slow to speak, careful not to get angry, not to worry what others might try to do toward us, seek only Godly honor.[cviii] A person who knows God and walks in the Spirit is not anxious, worried, or concerned, knowing that God empowers them with power, love, and self-discipline.[cix]

Biblical Self-Control

God created us to stand up for what we believe.[cx] God created us to be independent, self-disciplined, self-governing, and under control. Scripturally, at the core of this concept is a person with a strong godly life, seeing consistent spiritual growth, and reproducing godly fruit in themselves and others. If a person cannot govern what they think, say, or do; they are in danger of having out of control passions. They will have a hard time getting along with others. They will be on the outs with God. Their life will most likely be marked by major unrestrained behavioral issues.

God calls on us to behave in an orderly manner, be sober, serious, sane, sound-minded, discreet, self-disciplined, prudent, and moderate. The apostle Paul encouraged us not to think more highly of ourselves but to think soberly, based on our faith.[cxi]

A person who has self-control is even-handed and restrains their passions. They make proper use of their desires, and do not go to extreme on anything. A person reflecting this quality will make steady progress in the faith.[cxii]

In relationship to self-control, the writer of Proverbs 25 draws a picture of a city whose walls have been so utterly wrecked as to be without defense against an oncoming enemy. The comparison is an individual who has no restraint over their spirit, passions, or energies. They are vulnerable to the onslaught of anger, lust, and emotional disfunction that could destroy relationships, credibility, even their personality.[cxiii]

Then in Galatians 5, Paul writes how the fruit of the Spirit leads us to have a strong willpower. Putting it in terms we can relate to are passion, pleasure, harmony, patience, peacefulness, honesty, loyalty, humility, and finally restraint. He states that these emotions are not unlawful. However, author John W. Ritenbaugh in his article which addresses this specific passage asks the question, "why did Paul list them in that order?" [cxiv] The list begins with "love" and ends with "restraint," better known as "self-control." What was Paul's meaning? Does love cause all these other characteristics? Does walking in the Spirit lead to self-control? One Greek word *engkrateia*, a noun, can be translated into English as "control" or "temperance". In the Greek it can mean strong, strength, power, dominion, having power over, or being master of.[cxv] So it seems that God wants His people to be the masters of their emotions and stand up for what they believe. So it seems that God wants His people to be of courage, power, and love. So it seems that God wants His people to be self-governing, sensible, sober, restrained, and disciplined in all aspects of their life.

Secular Self-Determination

The world would have us believe that self-determination is a theory of human motivation. This theory holds that humans have three general needs that we must meet in order to function and grow. They are

- Relatedness (affiliation)
  - This means we have to be connected to others.
- Autonomy (self-sufficiency)
  - This means at the same time we have to be able to do things independent of others.
- Competency (ability)
  - This means we have to be able to control the outcomes and master our circumstances.

Christianity differs in its meaning to all these words. In relation to affiliation and being connected, we must relate to others and God. That connection is expressed in a love for others and for God. Christianity is structured in various levels of group assemblages from the small groups to denominations. Everything has to be centered around the person of Jesus Christ.

In relation to self-sufficiency it means freedom from a sinful nature through the sacrifice of Jesus Christ. On the other hand, that freedom is not without being dependent. Being dependent and reliant on God and an interaction with others in communion with Christ.

Ability is about hard work. The secular world would have us believe that one needs to work hard to get what you want (sluggards vs. industrious in proverbs). The Bible emphasizes character, work ethics, quality not quantity of work, all of which brings honor and glory to God.[cxvi]

Selfishness[cxvii]

We are warned in scripture against being selfish. We are told how it brings with it the evils of pride. Yet, we find it hard to detect such conduct and attitudes in ourselves. Often people with these characteristics overlook this shortcoming in themselves.[cxviii] Unless they have confidential friends who can bring this to their attention, they miss the warning signs of self-contempt, lack of humility, and arrogance. Pride is expressed and understood as thinking that we are the most important of all. It is the attitude that we are only loved, admired, and respected if we are seen as being above everyone else. It is an obsession of one's own value. Proverbs states such an attitude leads to destruction.[cxix] It goes on to say that pride is similar to a person who talks big but does not deliver.[cxx] A conceited, pretentious life is empty of substance.[cxxi] Scripture goes on to advise us not to argue with a person who thinks highly of themselves.[cxxii] It further says that calling attention to your own accomplishments is not wise.[cxxiii] Scripture goes on to offer profound wisdom on the topic of selfishness. We are warned of the temptation and perils of being selfish rather than generous and being helpful to our family and neighbors. We are told that a generous person prospers and that those who encourage others will be encouraged themselves.[cxxiv] We are commanded to be giving and kind rather than greedy and selfish. It will be hard to find happiness or success while being selfish. Selfishness only isolates us. It brings despair, depression, and darkness.

BIBLE STUDY

Proverbs 16:32
> Whoever is slow to anger is better than the mighty, and he who rules his spirit than he who takes a city.

2 Timothy 1:7
> For God gave us a spirit not of fear but of power and love and self-control.

Proverbs 25:28
> A man without self-control is like a city broken into and left without walls.

James 1:19
> Know this, my beloved brothers: let every person be quick to hear, slow to speak, slow to anger.

1 Corinthians 9:25
> Every athlete exercises self-control in all things. They do it to receive a perishable wreath, but we are imperishable.

1 Corinthians 9:27
> But I discipline my body and keep it under control, lest after preaching to others I myself should be disqualified.

1 Corinthians 10:24
> No one should seek their own good, but the good of others.

Matthew 20:25-28; Mark 10:42-45
> Jesus said, The princes of the Gentiles exercise dominion over them, and they exercise authority upon them. But it shall not be so among you whosoever will be great among you, let him be your minister. Whosoever will be chief among you, let him be your servant.

Please answer the following questions:
- What does self-control and servant leadership have in common?
- What are the qualities manifested by self-control?

POWER

BOLAND

POWER &
AUTHORITY
IN CONFLICT

The body is one and has many members,
though many, are one body,
so it is with Christ.
In one Spirit we were all baptized
In one body Jews or Greeks, slaves or free
all were made to drink of one Spirit.
For the body does not consist of one
member but of many.
1 Corinthians 12:12-31

JEWISH LEADERS

<u>Sanhedrin</u>

Sanhedrin is a Greek word for council or assembly, and such legal councils were common throughout Judea during the time of Christ. In Jesus time, power and control resided in the occupying Roman army. The Romans permitted the Jews a significant amount of self-government, which included the Sanhedrin as their court of law. The Sanhedrin consisted of a high priest and 22 respected (holy) men selected from other high priests, elders, heads of prominent families, plus scribes or lawyers (the establishment elite if you will). These individuals judged both civil and religious matters. In Jerusalem, there was a 71-member Sanhedrin with many responsibilities akin to those in local communities. Often referred to as the Greater Sanhedrin, this council had the added duties of deciding critical issues such as declaring war, resolving temple issues and adjudicating charges surrounding false prophets. They also served as a kind of supreme court within Judea. Its leader was the Temple high priest. Members were selected for life. According to the book of John, any Sanhedrin decision which called for capital punishment required justification and the passing of judgment by the occupying Roman governor.[cxxv]

The Origin of the Sanhedrin came out of the Book of Numbers, after Moses' complaint. God instructed him to select 70 elders from the group and then gave them some of the spirit he had bestowed on Moses. Many scholars say this is where the concept of the 71-member Sanhedrin originated.[cxxvi] They insisted on obedience to the Laws of Moses, including the additional oral traditions. They inflicted strict interpretations of the Law and demanded compliance with additional rules and unnecessary rituals. The Jerusalem Sanhedrin were a combination of political and religious parties of the time. The Pharisees being the most religious and the Sadducees the most political. Jesus often criticized the Pharisees due to their hypocrisy related to the interpretation and enforcement of the law. They took away the simple insight into what God said and how to apply it to life.[cxxvii]

Pharisees

Pharisees is a Greek word for "separated ones." This group viewed themselves as religiously superior to everyone else (proudful). The lawyer members of the Sanhedrin were Pharisees, experts on religious law. They believed that a messiah was coming and encouraged the people in this belief.

Sadducees

We don't know for sure how the name came about. A common belief is that it was derived from the name of prominent Old Testament High Priest, Zadok.[cxxviii] This group were the temple aristocracy. They advocated obedience and faithfulness to the written law while rejecting oral traditions. Unlike the Pharisees, they did not believe in life after death, angels or spirits. They were neither looking, for nor believed in, a messiah. They were known to have bribed the Roman authorities. In return many of their members were appointed to important roles, including Temple high priest, and thus controlled the Sanhedrin.

Initially, the Sadducees saw little threat from Jesus personally, his message, miracles, and special magnetism but as His popularity grew it became apparent that it could possibly produce public disorder or a revolution. The Gospel of John outlined the Sanhedrin's response. They believed let alone [Jesus], might stir up the people and cause the Romans to come and take away both the land and nation.[cxxix] The chief priest declared that it was better for one man to die, so that the whole nation not perish.[cxxx] If they did not take matters into their own hands the Romans would forcefully intervene and destroy the political status quo.[cxxxi]

<u>Essenes</u>

A third faction, the Essenes, emerged out of a disgust with the other two. This sect believed the others had corrupted the Word of God, the Temple, and the city of Jerusalem. They moved out of Jerusalem and lived a monastic life in the desert, adopting strict dietary laws and a commitment to celibacy. [cxxxii]

After looking at these so-called leaders of the day several questions come to mind.

1. What did Pharisees actually believe?

Pharisees believed in
- The resurrection of the dead and the afterlife.
- They believed like all Jews that God created the world.
- God chose Israel as His chosen people, rewarded and punished them according to His law.
- The law of Moses contained vague statements. Through the use of power and authority they believed they could fix these flaws by developing rules and regulations for every possible human action in order to adhere to what they thought was the Will of God as outlined in the Torah.

2. What do the Sadducees believe?

Sadducees believed that there was
- No resurrection of the dead,
- No afterlife,
- No spirit realm,
- No angels.

3. What did Jesus say about Pharisees?

Jesus at various times called Pharisees
- A brood of vipers,
- Compared them to Satan and called them hypocrites.
- Some pharisees even followed Him,
  - He praised these for following a righteous path.

4. What did the Pharisees believe that the Sadducees did not?

- Pharisees believed in the resurrection of the dead and an afterlife.
  - The Sadducees did not believe in either of these.
- The Pharisees believed in a realm of spirit and angels.
  - The Sadducees did not.

- Pharisees came from all economic classes but were distinguished by their rigid adherence to specific behavior prescriptions arising from their interpretation of the ambiguities in the Torah.[cxxxiii]
  - Sadducees were upper-class wealthy men mostly from Jerusalem who made up the Jewish aristocracy.

The Scripture exposes the people who were opposed to Jesus power and authority. His main antagonist were the scribes and Pharisees. In the book of Luke it tells us that these two groups sought to have Jesus arrested on several occasions.[cxxxiv] In the book of John we are told that they really wanted to stone Him.[cxxxv] Why?

- Jesus was loved by the people and associated with them.
  - The people loved Jesus. The people received Him gladly. The people felt judgment from the Pharisees. The Pharisees judged their sin. There was a mutual contempt. The Pharisees saw Jesus associating with the common people. The Pharisees saw

the people cheering Jesus and loving Him. The Pharisees couldn't stand it. They were envious and suspicious of His popularity, power, and authority.

- Jesus exposed them.
  - Jesus exposed the Pharisees as fake. Jesus was truth, His presence was genuine, righteousness, and holiness.
- The Pharisees were afraid of Jesus power and authority.

They weren't afraid of Him, so much of the consequences of what He could do. People in positions of power and authority fear losing that. The Jewish leaders feared the consequences of a revolt against Rome. They feared the Romans. They feared that Jesus somehow would lead an insurrection, cause another uprising, bring a bloodbath, and consequently they would lose their power and authority. So, they had to remove Him before He caused them trouble.[cxxxvi]

BIBLE STUDY

Mark 12:38-40, Luke 20:45-47

And he said unto them in His doctrine, Beware of the scribes, which love to go in long clothing, and love salutations in the marketplaces, and the chief seats in the synagogues, and the uppermost rooms at feasts, which devour widows' houses, and for a pretense make long prayers: these shall receive greater damnation.

Matthew 231-11

Then spoke Jesus to the multitude, and to His disciples. Saying the scribes and the Pharisees sit in Moses' seat.
- All therefore whatsoever they bid you observe, that observe and do, but do not you after their works. For they say, and do not.
- they bind heavy burdens and grievous to be borne and lay them on men's shoulders.
- They themselves will not move them with one of their fingers.
- their works they do for to be seen of men.
- They make broad their phylacteries
- They enlarge the borders of their garments and
- They love the uppermost rooms at feasts,

- They love the chief seats in the synagogues,
- They love greetings in the markets,
- They love to be called of men, Rabbi,

But be not you called Rabbi. For one is your Master, even Christ; and all you are brethren.

Call no man your father upon the earth for one is your Father, which is in heaven.

Neither be you called masters. For one is your Master, even Christ. But he that is greatest among you shall be your servant.

Matthew23:23-31

- Woe unto you, scribes and Pharisees, hypocrites! for you pay tithe of mint and anise and cummin, and have omitted the weightier matters of the law, judgment, mercy, and faith: these ought you to have done, and not to leave the other undone. You blind guides, which strain at a gnat, and swallow a camel.

- Woe unto you, scribes and Pharisees, hypocrites! for you make clean the outside of the cup and of the platter, but within they are full of extortion and excess. Thou blind Pharisee, cleanse first that which is within the cup and platter, that the outside of them may be clean also.

- Woe unto you, scribes and Pharisees, hypocrites! for you are like unto whited sepulchers, which indeed appear beautiful outward, but are within full of dead men's bones, and of all uncleanness. Even so you also outwardly appear righteous unto men, but within you are full of hypocrisy and iniquity.

- Woe unto you, scribes and Pharisees, hypocrites! because you build the tombs of the prophets, and garnish the sepulchers of the righteous, And say, If we had been in the days of our fathers, we would not have been partakers with them in the blood of the prophets. Wherefore you be witnesses unto yourselves, that you are the children of them which killed the prophets.

Please answer the following questions:
- Does Jesus really indicate that the religious leaders of that day abused their power and authority?
- Why was Jesus so harsh on the religious leaders of the day?
- Would Jesus be as critical of the religious leaders today?

The Battle Between Sovereignty and Self-Determination

cxxxvii

1. The Clarity of Words:

<u>Sovereignty</u> is when someone exercises supreme permanent power and authority. When someone is independent, with unmatched power. When someone has effective, absolute, authoritative, power and authority. When someone has supreme power. When someone has power over a body politic. When someone has freedom from external control. When someone is autonomous. When someone has controlling or influence over others.[cxxxviii]

<u>Self-determination</u> When someone has power and control over their own acts. A national state that has power and control within its borders without external coercion. Decisions made by people without outside

interference. When someone makes choices of their own free will.[cxxxix]

2. The Battle Over Words:

In the Church

Power interests within many denominations have clashed between differing viewpoints of when and how a believer believes. One group sides with John Calvin, the other with Jacob Arminius. It all boils down to whether a believer is chosen beforehand or self-determines (choice) when to come to Christ. Within that discussion is the idea of "self-control." Do "we" make the decision to come to Christ or did God make it for us at the beginning of time? What appears to be a simple decision for the individual based on a personal decision has been a matter long debated between power brokers for authority and control over religious faiths. We are talking about the control agents of religious thought! Within the upper religious circles one will hear the arguments between these two separate groups the Calvinist and the Arminian. Most of us don't know who or what they are. Most of us don't even understand their debate issues. However, at the heart of the debate is God's sovereign election versus human self-determination. In other words did you choose to come to Christ of your own free will or did God make that decision before the beginning of time?

John Calvin, (1509-1564) a French theologian and ecclesiastical statesman was the leading French Protestant reformer in the second generation of the Reformation.[cxl] His theory is called <u>Calvinism</u> and is all about "predestination." He believed the following:

- God already chose who will/will not be saved or go to heaven, and
- There is nothing a person can do to change God's decision.

Jacob Arminius (1560-1609) was a Dutch professor in theology at the University of Leiden. He led the opposition to Calvin's theory and his position is called <u>Arminianism</u> and is all about "self-determination."

- God only "calls" those whom He knows will accept Christ on their own.
- Jesus died for everyone, even those who are not chosen and will not believe.
- Everyone has the freedom of choice to accept/reject God's call to be saved.
- Believers can lose their salvation if they actively reject the Holy Spirit's influence in their lives. [cxli]

Want to start a good debate? Just lob this divisive subject into a large group of theologians and watch the fun begin.

In the Secular Society

Submission to an outside power and authority versus the idea of an independent self-rule is a real issue in the secular world. People groups do not always create their national boundaries. They therefore do not have sovereignty over their own choice of rulers, form of government, or status. People groups many times have a sense of loyalty to their own partisanship toward their group not their national boundary. Many national boundaries were arbitrarily created after some type of global or regional conflict and thus created the idea of a nation state. These new nations created unnatural borders among hostile neighbors. Unification among these diverse factions never occurred and might never happen. Unfortunately divisions have been deep and extreme. This idea of nationalism has, in some cases, fueled violence, division, and global disorder. As of 2022 the world recognized a significant number of national boundaries with this unfortunate separation.

One such group is the Kurds. The Kurdish people live in Iran, Iraq, Syria, and Turkey. These people do not have a country of their own and are a minority in all the countries that they inhabit. Their loyalty is to their culture not their nation state. In many instances they are considered terrorist for trying to demand recognition within each national boundary.

Belgium, on the other hand, is home to two different groups of people, Flemish and Walloons. Both have a distinct language and cultural identities. These two people groups live in harmony with each other.

Then there is Japan, it is made up of 98% of the same ethnicity, nearly all speak Japanese, nearly all share the same national traditions. The type of nationalism that calls for advancing the interests of one group above all else is ill advised and dangerous. This form of extremism is frightening, intolerant, and does not accept those outside the narrowly defined nation as equal. A few examples of this nationalized mentality are Nazi Germany, who attempted to eliminate the Jewish minority; and Modern-day China, who are currently attempting to eliminate the Muslim Uighurs.

BIBLE STUDY

James 3:16
> For where you have envy and selfish ambition, there you find disorder and every evil practice.

Proverbs 18:1
> An unfriendly person pursues selfish ends and against all sound judgment starts quarrels.

Romans 2:8
> But for those who are self-seeking and who reject the truth and follow evil, there will be wrath and anger.

2 Timothy 3:1-4
> This know also, that in the last days perilous times shall come. For men shall be lovers of their own selves, covetous, boasters, proud, blasphemers, disobedient to parents, unthankful, unholy, without natural affection, trucebreakers, false accusers, incontinent, fierce, despisers of those that are good, traitors, heady, high-minded, lovers of pleasures more than lovers of God.

Philippians 2:3-4

> Let nothing be done through strife or vainglory; but in lowliness of mind let each esteem other better than themselves. Look not every man on his own things, but every man also on the things of others

James 4:1-4

> From whence come wars and fighting among you? Come they not hence, even of your lusts that war in your members? You lust, and have not: you kill, and desire to have, and cannot obtain you fight and war, yet you have not, because you ask not. You ask, and receive not, because you ask amiss, that you may consume it upon your lusts. You adulterers and adulteresses, know you not that the friendship of the world is enmity with God? Whosoever therefore will be a friend of the world is the enemy of God.

Galatians 5:26

> Let us not be desirous of vain glory, provoking one another, envying one another.

Please answer the following questions:
- What seems to cause divisions?
- What could be done to settle divisions?

POWER

BOLAND

POWER &
AUTHORITY
LAST WORD

*Every word of God proves true;
He is a shield to those who take refuge in Him.
Do not add to His words, lest He rebuke you
and you be found a liar.*
                              Proverbs 30:5-6 ESV

WHO IS IN CHARGE, REALLY?

As a human race we are more concerned with our surroundings, our security, our future, our personal life than what is really important. We are divided over such things as philosophy, national origin, body parts, body functions, and government funding than what is more important. We posture ourselves between the logical and politically insane. We hate each other over unnecessary matters. We call each other names which hurt, insult, and humiliate. We should consider taking time to look at God's Word for a comprehensive statement of encouragement.[cxlii] It might help us to understand that we are all doing things wrong. It might make us realize that we do not have power, control, or authority over anything that we think we do.

In an exchange with His disciples in the temple from Matthew 24-25, Jesus makes the following points. It is here that some of the disciples seemed to be in awe of the buildings, size, and grandeur of the temple. Surprisingly, Jesus made the statement in a parable? See all this He declared! All this will be reduced to rubble someday there will be nothing left here. (in A.D. 70 the temple was, in fact, destroyed)[cxliii] He went on to say that not one stone will be left upon another! Then He developed a series of parables relating to the end times which not only explained what our priorities should be but indicated what motivates those in power and authority:

- Those in power are all about gaining territory and expressing their aggression.

- Those in power will do anything to retain their power and authority.
  - They will create wars and spread rumors of wars.[cxliv]
  - They will use their power to rise nation against other nations.[cxlv]
  - They will use their power to control the masses by keeping them in fear by manipulating an atmosphere of crime and lawlessness.[cxlvi]

- Those in power will show their distain and mock anything religious and the things of God.[cxlvii]
  - They will use their power both politically and religiously to give people a false truth and lead people from the truth of God's Word.[cxlviii]

Jesus went on to say that God wants His leaders to use their power and authority in a way that supports others:

- As servant mentors not power schemers.[cxlix]
- As one prepared for whatever happens.[cl]
- As a witness ready to give an answer for their hope, joy, and love.[cli]
- As a helper, showing compassion toward strangers, needy, orphans, and widows.[clii]
- As someone seeking only what is true, noble, right, pure, lovely, admirable, excellent, and praiseworthy.[cliii]
- As a blessing to others through their talent, education, upbringing, background, finances, and/or skills.
- As a discipler, mentoring others in God's ways.
- As a teacher, bringing future generations to a knowledge of God.[cliv]

BIBLE STUDY

Revelation 22:18-19

> I warn everyone who hears the words of the prophecy of this book: if anyone adds to them, God will add to him the plagues described in this book, and if anyone takes away from the words of the book of this prophecy, God will take away his share in the tree of life and in the holy city, which are described in this book.

James 1:27

> Pure religion and undefiled before God and the Father is this, To visit the fatherless and widows in their affliction, and to keep himself unspotted from the world.

Philippians 4:8

> Finally, brethren, whatsoever things are true, whatsoever things are honest, whatsoever things are just, whatsoever things are pure, whatsoever things are lovely, whatsoever things are of good report; if there be any virtue, and if there be any praise, think on these things.

2 Timothy 2:2

> And the things that thou hast heard of me among many witnesses, the same commit thou to faithful men, who shall be able to teach others also.

Please answer the following questions:
- What is God's idea of man's authority and power?
- What is God's idea of the problem with man's use of power?

POWER

BOLAND

POWER &
AUTHORITY
PERSPECTIVE

Then He said to them:
These are My Words that I spoke to you
while I was still with you,
that everything written…must be fulfilled.
Luke 24:44

OLD TESTAMENT

With God's release of Israel toward human rule things did not turn out the way the people had hoped they would, but events did play out just as God had predicted. The first four Kings of the United Kingdom (c 1025-925 B.C.) were as follows:

- Saul, he did evil in God's sight and died in battle.[clv]
- Ishbosheth, Saul's son was temporarily put on the throne but eventually overthrown and assassinated.[clvi]
- King David was considered a man after God's own heart even though he was flawed[clvii].
- Solomon, the son from David and Bathsheba, did right in his youth but did evil in old age. [clviii]

  After his death the kingdom split with Judah (c 925-586 b.c.) going one way and Israel (c 925-721 BC) going another.

Judah's kings were as follows:

- Rehoboam was known for his arrogance.[clix]
- Abijam(AKA Abijah) who also did evil.
- They were followed by two righteous kings Asa, and Jehoshaphat.

- Jehoram (AKA Joram) killed his brothers, ignored God, and his bowels fell out.[clx]

- Ahaziah (AKA Azariah or Jehoahaz) listened to his idol worshipping mother.[clxi]

- Queen Athaliah she took over after the death of her son, she was evil, and eventually was killed in street by the people.[clxii]

- Joash (AKA Jehoash) is known as virtuous[clxiii]

- Amaziah sought help from other deities and he too was killed by own people.[clxiv]

- Uzziah (AKA Azariah) and Jotham both did right by God.[clxv]

- Ahaz was an idol worshiper and sacrificed own sons.[clxvi]

- Hezekiah was very righteous.[clxvii]

- King Manasseh did evil before God.[clxviii] he repented toward the end of his life. [clxix]

- King Amon was proud, an idol worshipper and was finally killed by his servants.[clxx]

- King Josiah was righteous.

The last four Kings of Judah were evil:

- Jehoahaz (AKA Shallum) the Egyptian Pharoah killed him. [clxxi]

- Jehoiakim (AKA Eliakim) ignored Jeremiah's warning, was taken to

Babylon, and was considered a degenerate.[clxxii]

- Jehoiachin (AKA Coniah or Jeconiah) was an idol worshipper and also exiled to Babylon.[clxxiii]
- Zedekiah (AKA Mattaniah) was a puppet of Babylon, an idol worship, and caused Jerusalem to be leveled.[clxxiv]

The first ten kings of Israel all did evil in the sight of God:[clxxv]

- Jeroboam, Nadab was assassinated.
- Baasha was assassinated.
- Elah was assassinated.
- Zimri committed suicide.
- Tibni, Omri considered most evil.
- Ahab with Queen Jezebel worshiped Baal.
- Ahaziah died of injury.
- Jehoram (AKA Joram).
- King Jehu had mixed reviews.

Then there came another series of evil kings:[clxxvi]

- Jehoahaz,
- Joash (AKA Jehoash),
- Jeroboam II.

Finally, the remaining kings were also evil, this included kings: [clxxvii]

- Zachariah, Shallum, Menahem, Pekahiah, Pekah and Hoshea.

By the end of the 4th Century B.C. the promised land was no longer controlled by the people God called. They ignored Him. They no longer paid attention to Him. The people of God were dispersed throughout the known world. The ruling class no longer considered God in any way in their decision making. However, the people got their way, they were just like every other nation.

SECULAR WORLD

By the time of Christ, war was the common denominator in gaining authority and establishing a new ruling class. New forms of government began developing such as:

- Anarchy (each individual had their own power and authority, no laws, or no overall governance)

- Confederation (loose union of individual identified states which had retained their separate power and authority)
    - 19th Century Germany
    - Modern Switzerland
    - British Commonwealth of Nations,
    - U.S. Articles of Confederation (1781–89)
    - French Community

- Unitary (All power and authority lie in a central governmental structure)

- Federation (power and authority divided between identifiable political entities within the organization structure)

- Empire (All power and authority are under a dominant ruler)
    - Macedonian, Assyrian, Babylonian, Ptolemaic, Ming, Ottoman, Roman, British, Mongolian, & Russian

- Theocracy (All power and authority entrusted to a religious organization or religious head and its priestly hierarchy)
  - Roman Catholic Church

- Feudalism (What power and authority there is controlled by those who own the land)

- Monarchy (All power and authority given and passed down through a designated royal family)

- Democracy (The power and authority originates and retained by the people yet handed over to representatives to establish rule of law.)

In his book "The Creators", author Daniel J. Boorstin gives a compelling argument that Philo of Alexander a prominent Egyptian philosopher changed the course of Christian thought and theology. Philo was the leading representative of Hellenistic-Jewish thought of his day and strongly attracted to Greek philosophy. When debating against the Greek philosophers, he based his arguments on Christian beliefs. He believed that the love of God allowed man to become filled with "god-like" qualities such as power and authority.[clxxviii]

He would go on to say that man had the potential to be a "creator." Man could throw off their Greek stereotype of being a victim of the gods of Greek mythology. His discourses developed the idea of "Christian theology". Whether intentional or not, out of this theological thought grew the religious organization we recognize today. The idea of church with structure, design, and intention. This was the turning point that brought together all the early century theories floating around in Christendom about, such as:

- What do the Gospels really mean?
- What is the nature of man?
- What is man's relationship to God?
- What is God's relationship to the governance of the nations?
- What is meant by the end of times?
- What does it mean to be saved?

Philo's problem was that he respected Plato way too much and many critics took his thoughts on Christianity as dabbling with mythology. However, that did not stop his theories from being carried forward as "truth."

So, how did his theories affect the discipleship group Christ establish? Over time it morphed into an organization of an "elite group" based on their ability to maintain their power and control. At some point in time these power brokers limited access to the written word concerning Christ's intentions. Then they devised criteria for those who might want to try and fully comprehend, debate, and understand God's Word. They also established standards for the requirements of church "membership" (i.e.: baptism).[clxxix] Then came the collapse of the Roman Empire. The newly formed Catholic Church developed into a quasi-government and negotiated the collapse of Rome, and resulting "so-called" conversion of tribal barbarians and others to Christianity. For the next several decades the "church" had complete power and authority approximately A.D. 300 to 1500.

BOLAND

BIBLE STUDY

Romans 13:1

> Let every soul be subject unto the higher powers. For there is no power but of God: the powers that be are ordained of God.

1 Peter 2:13-14

> Submit yourselves to every ordinance of man for the Lord's sake: whether it be to the king, as supreme; or unto governors, as unto them that are sent by him for the punishment of evildoers, and for the praise of them that do well.

Romans 13:6-7

> For this cause pay your tribute also: for they are God's ministers, attending continually upon this very thing. Render therefore to all their dues: tribute to whom tribute is due; custom to whom custom; fear to whom fear; honor to whom honor.

Please answer the following questions:

- What perspective do these verses put on how we should view government?
- What was God's view of government?

POWER

BOLAND

CONCLUSION

So, God has all power and authority. He created everything from that power and authority. He even created man in his image. He created them for a relationship with the free will to choose. He chose one particular group of people to have a relationship with through Abraham. He chose to communicate His Will, His Desire, and His Authority with these descendants through His Prophets. He led these people from slavery to freedom. Eventually their descendants decided they wanted to look just like other people and be controlled by other men rather than God. He warned them of the hazards. They would not listen. Even so, God would yield to that request to have someone in charge other than Him. He knew full well what such a move would unleash onto the world but He did it anyway.

God gave them a king. Successive kings ruled both good, bad, and indifferent. Eventually other forms of government followed. All these forms of government did exactly as God had warned the people. Each new government became worse and worse. This man-made power and authority ultimately took over religion and fulfilled God's prediction there too. God eventually backed away from communicating with the people. He even sent His Son in an attempt of restoring His relationship with man. Those who controlled the power and authority over the religion of the day killed His Son thinking they were doing the right thing. God's plans did not die but were fulfilled and man's future was sealed. God's prediction of man's rule continued to play out. So, we see young men and women being forced into military service, we see people being forced into labor camps for political purposes, we see the creation of excessive taxes, the building up of huge national debts, governments taking over private property for their purposes, governments redistributing that property for their uses, governments creating unrestrained political power based on their undisciplined authority. As God said, as God warned, and so it came true.

The conclusion of this message is that you would understand the absolute authority and sovereignty that God left us through His son Jesus Christ. You must understand this whatever age you are,

- You must understand even if you are in your 20's and just finishing college, beginning that career, or about to get married or still single.

- You must understand even if you are in your 30's and just getting the hang of a career.

- You must understand even if you are in your 40's and at the height your career or in a midlife crisis.

- You must understand even if you are in your 50's and entrenched in the career battle of your life, facing aging parents, or an empty nester.

- You must understand even if you are in your 60's and seeing the end of your career coming soon, lost a loved one and facing life alone.

- You must understand even if you are in your 70's facing the reality of the American dream.

- You must understand even if you are past 80 years and facing your own mortality.

Fact:
>God has all power and authority!
>God turned this world over to human rule.
>Decisions carry with them consequences!

Now that we know these facts, what should our response be when we disagree with human power and authority?
- ✓ Should we question and rebel?
  - o Like Adam and Eve?[clxxx]
- ✓ Should we act out violently?
  - o Like Cain against Able?[clxxxi]
- ✓ Should we attempt to overthrow legitimate power and authority?
  - o Like Aaron and Mariam[clxxxii]
- ✓ Should we defer to the legitimate power and authority?
  - o Like David toward King Saul[clxxxiii]

Understand this, God's law must be obeyed rather than man's law, if they are in conflict.[clxxxiv] As the Egyptian midwives dis when they refused to kill the newborn Jewish children under Pharoah's order. As the Jewish leaders did when they refused to bow down before idols under the King's degree. We must declared to those in power and authority.

>*...be it known unto thee, O king,*
>*that we will not serve thy gods, nor worship*
>*the golden image which thou hast set up.*[clxxxv]

At the end of the book of Matthew, Jesus explained His power and authority and what He expects of His followers. He said, "All authority in heaven and on earth has been given to me. Therefore:

1. Go (and as we are going),

    a. Make disciples of all nations,

    b. Baptize new believers (in the name of the Father, Son, and Holy Spirit),

    c. Teach them (to observe all that Jesus commanded),

2. Behold, Jesus is always with us (to the end of the age).

So are we accepting the power and authority that God gave us through Christ?

- Are we making and baptizing new believers?

- Are we teaching them to know the scriptures?

- Do they understand our responsibilities?

- Are we making, baptizing and teaching new believers themselves?

- Or are we paralyzed, worried, and anxious over by the use and abuse that human governments have mismanaged with their legitimate power and authority?

POWER

BIBLE STUDY

Matthew 28:18-20

Jesus came and spoke unto them, saying, All power is given unto me in heaven and in earth. Go ye therefore, and teach all nations, baptizing them in the name of the Father, and of the Son, and of the Holy Ghost: Teaching them to observe all things whatsoever I have commanded you: and, lo, I am with you always, even unto the end of the world. Amen.

2 Timothy 1:7

For God hath not given us the spirit of fear; but of power, and of love, and of a sound mind.

Please answer the following question:

- What did Paul mean by a spirit of power rather than fear?

POWER

BOLAND

BIBLIOGRAPHY

<hr>

INTRODUCTION

[i] 2 Samuel 22:33 , 2 Chronicles 20:6, Job 26:7-14, Psalm 71:18, 147:4-5, Jeremiah 10:12-13, Daniel 2:20-22, 4:17, 2 Timothy 3:16-17, 2 Peter 1:21, Revelation 11:17

[ii] Genesis 1:1

[iii] Genesis 1:3

[iv] Genesis 1:4-5

[v] Genesis 1:6-10

[vi] Genesis 1:11-13

[vii] Genesis 1:20-31

[viii] https://www.hebrewversity.com/hebrew-origins-adams-name-connection-ground/

[ix] https://creation.com/five-things-about-eve
https://weekly.israelbiblecenter.com/eve-mean-hebrew/

[x] Job 26:7

[xi] Isaiah 40:22

[xii] John 1:3

[xiii] Isaiah 45:18

POWER RECOGNIZED

[xiv] Deuteronomy 5

[xv] Exodus 20:12, Ephesians 5:22-33, 2 Corinthians 6:14, Matthew 5:28, Hebrews 10:24-25, 1 Corinthians 13:4-7, 1 Corinthians 15:33, Ecclesiastes 4:9-12, Psalm 10:14, Exodus 22:21-24, Isaiah 1:17, James 1:27, Job 29:12-17 Jeremiah 7:6-7 & 49:11 Matthew 25:31-46
1 Thessalonians 5:11,

[xvi] Matthew 26:39, 42; Luke 22:42; John 5:19, 30

[xvii] John 14:26, 15:26, Acts 1:8

[xviii] Ephesians 5:21–6:4; Proverbs 6:20–21

[xix] Galatians 6:2; Hebrews 10:24–25; Psalm 133:1

[xx] John 14:26, 15:26; Acts 1:8; Ephesians 4:11–16, Hebrews 13:17; I Peter 5:1–11

[xxi] Colossians 3:22–4:1;I Peter 2:18

[xxii] Matthew 20:25-28

[xxiii] What are God-ordained authority structures? Structures of Authority order in the home, church, workplace, and government, Institute in Basic Life Principles https://iblp.org/questions/what-are-god-ordained-authority-structures

[xxiv] Isaiah 55:8-9

[xxv] *What are God-ordained authority structures? Structures of Authority order in the home, church, workplace, and government, Institute in Basic Life Principles* https://iblp.org/questions/what-are-god-ordained-authority-structures

[xxvi] Romans 13:1

[xxvii] I Peter 2:13–17 and Romans 13:1–5

[xxviii] Matthew 20:25-28; Colossians 3:23–24

[xxix] Deuteronomy 27:26-28:1-2

[xxx] Genesis 2:18, Ephesians 5:21–6:4, Proverbs 6:20–21

[xxxi] Genesis 6:1-3, Proverbs 6:20-21

[xxxii] 1 Corinthians 6:16–20

[xxxiii] Genesis 2:24, Ephesians 5:21

[xxxiv] *Catholic bishops approve new guidance on Communion for pro-abortion rights politicians,* The bishops did not single out President Joe Biden by name. By Matthew Vann (2022) https://abcnews.go.com/Politics/catholic-bishops-approve-guidance-communion-pro-abortion-rights/story?id=81206649 Some religions support abortion rights. Their leaders are speaking up. *"We support abortion justice not despite our religious values but because of them."* By Julianne McShane (2022) https://www.nbcnews.com/news/us-news/religions-support-abortion-rights-leaders-are-speaking-rcna27194

[xxxv] I Peter 2:13–17, Romans 13:1–5

[xxxvi] Deuteronomy 10:17 (ESV), James 2:9 (ESV), Leviticus 19:15 (ESV), Romans 2:11 (ESV),

[xxxvii] Daniel 2:21, Psalm 109:8, Hosea 4:6

[xxxviii] Genesis 6:5-13

[xxxix] Genesis 1: 26–28, 2: 4b –24

[xl] *Structure of man in the biblical act of Creation*

December 2012 Analecta Cracoviensia 44:191 DOI:10.15633/acr.15 By Cardinal Stefan Wyszynski University in Warsaw https://www.researchgate.net/publication/280209239_Structure_of_man_in_the_biblical_act_of_Creation

xli *A Theory of Human Motivation* Paperback by Abraham H. Maslow, Martino Fine Books (2013)

xlii Ephesians 4:11–16, Hebrews 13:17, and I Peter 5:1–11

xliii Leviticus 19:13

xliv Colossians 3:22–4:1, I Peter 2:18

xlv Colossians 4:1

xlvi Colossians 3:22–25, I Peter 2:18

xlvii Genesis 2:15

xlviii Exodus 35:10, 35; Exodus 31:3-5; Proverbs 22:29; 1 Corinthians 12:4-6; 1 Peter 4:10-11

xlix Luke 19:13; 1 Timothy 5:18; James 5:4

l Deuteronomy 25:13; Proverbs 11:1, 22:16; Jeremiah 22:13; Job 31:13

li Psalm 112:5

PARADISE LOST

lii Genesis 3

liii *Challenging God's Authority by* Parkey Cobern (2019) https://pcobern.wordpress.com/2019/05/20/challenging-gods-authority/

liv Mark 1:21-22

lv Genesis 11:1–9

lvi Genesis 18:22-33

lvii Amos 7:1-7

lviii Habakkuk 1; Lamentation 2; The lament in Psalms.

lix 1Samuel 8:3-22

lx Isaiah 44:1

lxi Exodus 19:6

lxii Genesis 12:3

lxiii Genesis 26:3-5, 17:21; 26:24; 28:1-4, 13; Deuteronomy 7:7-8; 9:6;

lxiv Deuteronomy 34:10

---

lxv Romans 13:1-3

lxvi *The Challenge to Moses' Authority (Numbers 12)*
Bible Commentary / Produced by TOW Project
https://www.theologyofwork.org/old-testament/numbers-
and-work/the-challenge-to-moses-authority-numbers-12

lxvii *Jesus' Authority Questioned (Mark 11:27-33)*
Analysis and Commentary
https://www.learnreligions.com/jesus-authority-questioned-
248734

lxviii Proverbs 17:7, 1 John 1:6

lxix 1Samuel 8:9-17
    https://www.trinityfoundation.org/journal.php?id=13

lxx 1Samuel 8:18

lxxi *War in the Middle Ages,* Autumn 2005, Rachel Fulton,
Department of History, The University of Chicago
https://home.uchicago.edu/~rfulton/war.html

lxxii Code of Hammurabi, History.com Editors
https://www.history.com/topics/ancient-history/hammurabi
May 31, 2022, Publisher: A&E Television Networks
Updated, September 9, 2021,
Original Published Date: November 9, 2009

lxxiii Numbers 1:2-3

lxxivRomans 13:1-7, Colossians 1:16, 1 Peter 2:13-17,

lxxv Romans 12:19, 13:4, 1 Peter 3:9, 1 Thessalonians 5:15, 2
Thessalonians 1:8, Deuteronomy 32:35, Hebrews10:30,
Leviticus 19:18, Mark 11:25, Psalm 94:1-2, Proverbs 20:22,
24:29, Matthew 18:21-22,5:38-39, Ephesians

lxxvi 1 John 4:18, Romans 13:4

lxxvii Romans 6:16

lxxviii Romans 5:1-5, James 1:2-4

lxxix Romans 12:1-3, Philippians 4:6-7

lxxx Ephesians 6:9

lxxxi Esther 4:14

lxxxii James 5:12, Matthew 5:34, 36, 23:16-22, 26:74

lxxxiii Acts 19:13-16

lxxxiv Matthew 4:7

lxxxv *The Draft,* History.com (2020) (2017)

---

https://www.history.com/topics/us-government/conscription
[lxxxvi] https://bible.knowing-jesus.com/words/Drafted
https://bible.knowing-jesus.com/topics/Military-Service
[lxxxvii] Numbers 1:3
[lxxxviii] Psalm 144:1
[lxxxix] Deuteronomy 7, Joshua 6-12
[xc] Judges 20-21
[xci] Judges 6-7
[xcii] 1 Samuel 9 – 2 Samuel 21
[xciii] Exodus 22:18-24, Deuteronomy 27:19, Psalm 68:5, Isaiah 1:17, Zechariah 7:9-10, James 1:27, 2:14-17
[xciv] Psalm 68:5, Isaiah 1:17, Jeremiah 22:3,
[xcv] 1 Timothy 5:3-16

POWER EXPOSED

[xcvi] Acts 1:8
[xcvii] Matthew 5:43-44
[xcviii] Luke 10:19
[xcix] 2 Corinthians 12:9
[c] Hebrews 4:12
[ci] Matthew 4:4, 1 Corinthians 1:18, Romans 1:20, 2 Timothy 3:16;
[cii] James 5:13, 15-16, Mark 11:24
[ciii] James 1:22
[civ] 2 Timothy 3:5
[cv] John 3:16-17
[cvi] Romans 8:11, Ephesians 3:20-21, Hebrews 2:18,
[cvii] Proverbs 25:28
[cviii] Proverbs 16:32, 2 Timothy 1:7, Proverbs 25:28, James 1:19, 1 Corinthians 9:25, 27
[cix] 2 Timothy 1:7
[cx] James 1:12, 1 Corinthians 16:13
[cxi] Romans 12:3; see Titus 2:6; I Peter 4:7
[cxii] *Five Teachings of Grace,* by John W. Ritenbaugh Forerunner, "Personal," (1996) https://www.cgg.org/index.cfm/library/article/id/478/five-teachings-of-grace.htm

---

[cxiii] Proverbs 25:28
[cxiv] *The Fruit of the Spirit*, by John W. Ritenbaugh
Forerunner, "Personal," February 1998
https://www.cgg.org/index.cfm/library/article/id/294/the-fruit-of-spirit.htm
[cxv] Lexicon :: Strong's G1466 - egkrateia
https://www.blueletterbible.org/lexicon/g1466/esv/mgnt/0-1/
Eating: How Good It Is! (Part Six) by John W. Ritenbaugh
https://www.bibletools.org/index.cfm/fuseaction/Topical.show/RTD/cgg/ID/2735/Engkrateia.htm
[cxvi] *Theory of Self Determination and Christianity,* by Bradley Wright (2012)
https://www.patheos.com/blogs/blackwhiteandgray/2012/11/theory-of-self-determination-and-christianity/
[cxvii] Proverbs 29:2 ESV
[cxviii] Matthew 7:1-5, Luke 6:37-42
[cxix] Proverbs 16:18, 18:12
[cxx] Proverbs 25:14
[cxxi] Proverbs 13:7a
[cxxii] Proverbs 26:12
[cxxiii] Proverbs 27:2
[cxxiv] Proverbs 11:25

POWER IN CONFLICT

[cxxv] John 18:31
[cxxvi] Numbers 11:16-26
[cxxvii] Luke 11:52
[cxxviii] 2 Samuel 15:23-29; 1 Kings 2:35
[cxxix] John 11:47-48
[cxxx] John 11: 49-50
[cxxxi] John 11:53
[cxxxii] *Ancient Jewish History: Pharisees, Sadducees & Essenes*
https://www.jewishvirtuallibrary.org/pharisees-sadducees-and-essenes
[cxxxiii] https://study.com/learn/lesson/pharisees-sadducees.html

cxxxiv Luke 20
cxxxv John 5,8,10
cxxxvi *Why Did the Pharisees Hate Jesus So Much? By* R.C. Sproul
https://www.ligonier.org/posts/why-did-pharisees-hate-jesus-so-much
cxxxvii Ephesians 1:3-14
cxxxviii The American Heritage College Dictionary, 3rd Edition, Houghton-Mifflin, Boston (1993)
cxxxix The American Heritage College Dictionary, 3rd Edition, Houghton-Mifflin, Boston (1993)
cxl https://calvin.edu/about/history/john-calvin.html
cxli http://www.eloquorium.com/2010/06/03/sovereignty-vs-self-determination-eph13-14/
The Spirit of Babylon
CGG Weekly by David C. Grabbe
https://www.cgg.org/index.cfm/library/weekly/id/941/spirit-babylon-part-three.htm
Ecclesiastes Resumed (Part Twenty-Seven)
Sermon by John W. Ritenbaugh
https://www.cgg.org/index.cfm/library/sermon/id/3495/ecclesiastes-resumed-part-twenty.htm
Letting Go (Part One)
Sermonette by Joseph B. Baity

LAST WORD

cxlii 1 Thessalonians 5:11
cxliii https://www.myjewishlearning.com/article/the-temple-its-destruction/
© The Jewish Way.
cxliv Matthew 24:6
cxlv Matthew 24:7
cxlvi Matthew 24:12
cxlvii Matthew 24:15
cxlviii Matthew 24:5, 24
cxlix Matthew 20:28, 23:11; Mark 9:35, 10:44-45 ; John 13:12-14; 1 Peter 4:10

cl Matthew 25:1-12, 13

cli 1 Peter 3:15

clii Matthew 25:34-46; James 1:27; 1 John 3:17; Psalm 146:9; 1 Timothy 5:3; Hebrews 13:1-25; Mark 12:40

cliii Philippians 4:8

cliv Matthew 25:14-30

clv 1 Samuel 15:16-35, 31:5

clvi 2 Samuel 2:8-4:12

clvii Acts 13:22

clviii 2 Samuel 12:24, 1 Kings 11:9

clix 2 Chronicles 12:1

clx 2 Chronicles 21:19

clxi 2 Chronicles 20:35, 2 Kings 11:1

clxii 2 Kings 11:13-20

clxiii 2 Kings 12:2

clxiv 2 Chronicles 25:14

clxv 2 Chronicles 26:4,27:2

clxvi 2 Chronicles 28:1, 3

clxvii 2 Kings 18:1-3

clxviii 2 Chronicles 33:2

clxix 2 Chronicles 33:18-19

clxx 2 Chronicles 33:24

clxxi 2 Kings 23:34, 2 Chronicles 36:4

clxxii 2 Kings 23:34, Jeremiah 36:30-32

clxxiii Jeremiah 52:31

clxxiv 2 Kings 24:17, 20, 25:7

clxxv 2 Kings 10:29, 31

clxxvi 2 Kings 13:1-2, 2 Kings 12:18-20, 2 Kings 10:29

clxxvii 2 Kings 15:9, 18, 24, 35, 17:1-3

clxxviii 2 Timothy 1:7

clxxix *The Popes*, Antonio Lopes, Translation: Charles Nopar, Futura Edizioni (1997)
The Medici, Editors: Monica Fintoni, Andrea Paoletti, Giunti Industrie Grafiche, Prato (1999)

clxxx Genesis 3:1-7

clxxxi Genesis 4:8

clxxxii Genesis 12:1-9

---

clxxxiii 1 Kings 16-31
clxxxiv Acts 5:29
clxxxv Daniel 3:18